Data Engineering Unlocked

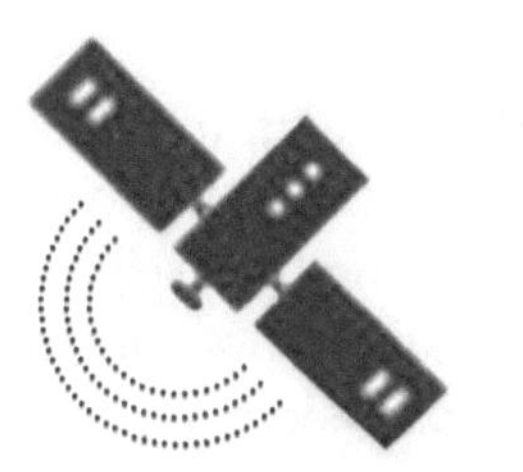

Foundation and Real World Insights of a High-Demand Field

Rakesh G

ISBN
Paperback 979-8-89744-773-2
Hardcase 979-8-89744-815-9

Dedication

Dedicated to The relentless problem solvers, the architects of data, and the visionaries who transform raw information into knowledge.

To the *Data Engineering community—past*, present, and *future*—who push the boundaries of technology and make sense of the ever-growing world of data.

May this book serve as a guiding light, unlocking new perspectives and empowering you to build systems that shape the future.

Keep learning. Keep innovating. Keep unlocking possibilities.

Contents

Part 3: Foundations and Mindsets for Data Engineering

Foreword

In today's digital age, data is the fundamental driver of innovation and business success. As a Data Architect, I've seen how data engineering is essential to building robust systems—spanning from real-time analytics to large-scale enterprise infrastructures.

When I came across *"Data Engineering Unlocked"*, I was immediately struck by its ability to break down the complexities of data engineering in a way that anyone can understand. This book doesn't just focus on the technicalities—it takes you on a journey through the real-world applications and deep impact data engineering has across industries. Whether you're new to the field or looking to broaden your understanding, this book is a perfect starting point.

What I truly appreciate about this book is its approach. It's not just about learning the tools and technologies; it's about seeing the bigger picture and understanding how data engineering fits into the larger puzzle of business and society. The real-world examples and stories shared in this book capture how data engineering isn't just a job—it's a craft that changes how we live and work.

Reading this book, you'll come to realize that data engineering isn't just about building systems—it's about creating the foundation for the future. This book will equip you with the mindset and the knowledge to think critically, solve problems creatively, and see how data can be used as a powerful tool to drive change.

It's a privilege to share this book with you, and I hope it sparks your curiosity, inspires your learning, and motivates you to unlock the endless possibilities data engineering has to offer.

Sincerely,
Venkatesh Muthukumarasamy
Data Architect, Cognizant technology solutions.

Foreword

In the world of data-driven decision-making, the role of data engineering cannot be overstated. As a Senior Data Analyst at Fiserv, I've witnessed firsthand how clean, reliable, and well-structured data pipelines empower analysts and decision-makers to unlock insights that drive business success. Without the foundation built by data engineers, much of what we do as analysts would not be possible.

What sets **"Data Engineering Unlocked"** apart is its focus on foundational principles and real-world applications. This book takes complex concepts and presents them in a way that is accessible to beginners while still being insightful for seasoned professionals. It highlights the true essence of data engineering: enabling innovation, solving complex problems, and creating systems that scale effortlessly.

For anyone curious about how data shapes industries or looking to build a career in this high-demand field, this book is an essential guide. It inspires readers to approach data engineering not just as a technical role but as a craft that drives impact across businesses and society.

It's an honor to introduce this book, which I believe will serve as both an inspiration and a resource for future engineers, analysts, and innovators alike.

Sincerely,
Vignesh R
Senior Data Analyst, Fiserv.

Foreword

In today's data-driven world, the ability to harness, process, and analyze data has transformed how businesses operate, innovate, and thrive. As industries continue to rely on data as their competitive advantage, the role of data engineers has emerged as not just important but indispensable. With over a decade of experience in this field, I have witnessed firsthand how the landscape of data engineering has evolved and shaped industries across the globe.

When I first learned about this book, **"Data Engineering Unlocked"**, I was struck by its mission: to demystify data engineering for beginners while inspiring professionals to explore its deeper potential. What makes this book unique is its ability to balance foundational principles with practical insights, presenting the field in a way that is accessible, actionable, and engaging.

I've had the privilege of witnessing the transformative impact of data engineering firsthand. From optimizing supply chains and enabling real-time analytics to designing scalable systems that power global enterprises, I've seen how skilled data engineers solve complex problems and unlock new opportunities. This book captures that essence beautifully, making it a must-read for anyone stepping into or curious about the field.

The author's approach to blending real-world examples with timeless principles ensures that this book is not just a guide but a resource that evolves with its readers. Whether you're a beginner eager to break into the field or an experienced professional looking to strengthen your foundational understanding, this book provides a roadmap for success.

As you turn these pages, I encourage you to not only absorb the technical knowledge but also embrace the mindset of curiosity and lifelong learning that this book so passionately advocates. Data engineering is more than a profession—it's a craft that shapes the future of businesses and society.

I'm delighted to introduce this book to you. I hope it inspires and equips you to unlock the limitless possibilities of data engineering.

Sincerely,
Vivekanand S
Senior Data Engineer.

Introduction

ata Engineering is the back-bone of our Data-driven world, however still it remains a mystery for many people. Have you ever thought about how businesses like E-commerce predict what we'll buy next?. Or how healthcare systems analyze patient data in real time? That's data engineering in action. But where do you begin if you want to step into this exciting and high-demand field?

This book is for anyone who is interested in learning more about the potential of data engineering for their projects, whether they are experienced professionals, beginners checking out this growing field, aspiring Data engineers or industry leaders.

This book will guide you regardless of who you are, whether you're new for data engineering, or managing a team exploring new projects, or just curious about the future of this field. Together, we are going to look at basic principles, Real Time applications and emerging trends that make data engineering a transformative field.

The world runs on data. This book unlocks the door to understanding and mastering the systems that bring it to life.

Part 1: Understanding the Foundations

Chapter 1

What is Data Engineering?

Defining Data Engineering: The Hidden Backbone of Our Digital World:

Have you ever wondered how a music app knows what song to play next, or how you get live traffic updates in maps during your morning commute? Behind all these there is a fascinating, yet overlooked field: Data engineering. It is not heard by everyone like data science or AI, but without it, the entire data-driven ecosystem cannot survive.

When I initially started learning about Data Engineering, I was totally struck by how integral it is to almost everything we rely on today. If you think of the world of data as a sprawling city, data engineers are the ones building the tunnels, bridges and highways that keep everything connected. But unlike physical infrastructure, these "roads" must adapt to an ever-changing landscape, processing massive amounts of information at speeds that would boggle the mind.

Basically, Data Engineering is about creating the systems that prepare, transforming messy, unstructured Data into clean and organized information. Let me share an example, when Netflix suggests your next favorite show automatically, it's because data engineers have built pipelines that process your viewing habits, genre preferences, and even time of day to deliver personalized recommendations in milliseconds.

But let's take a little step back. We should think Why is this so important? Without data engineers, analysts and data scientists would spend most of their time just wrangling data instead of doing what they're good at: finding patterns, making predictions, and solving problems. To tell precisely, it will be like trying to build a house without pre-cut wood or nails. Data engineers are the ones who provide those ready-to-use materials.

The Role of Data Engineers in Shaping the Modern World:

Data engineers are the heroes behind the scenes of the modern world in the era of digitalization. It is the personalized recommendations that one gets on a streaming platform, the navigation systems that assist drivers to find the best routes, or the inventory management systems for e-commerce to name a few, which are made possible by data engineers.

Imagine the complexity of E-commerce platforms like Amazon. Millions of products and customers, thousands of sellers all interacting in real-time. These operations will cease without data engineers ensuring that everything runs smoothly.

Data Infrastructure build and maintained by them which allows the businesses to:

> Have an Idea about customer preferences.

> Optimize operations.

> Identify trends before they happen.

Data engineers are the one who connects raw data with the applications that rely on it, making them essential in the modern world.

Data Engineering vs. Data Science and Data Analysis

There is always an overlap in discussion among the roles of data engineers, data scientists, and data analysts, but they're fundamentally different:

> Data Engineers are responsible for building and maintaining the infrastructure that collects, stores, and processes data. Their focus is on the systems and workflows that make data usable.

> ➤ Data Scientists use this clean, organized data to develop models, run experiments, and generate insights. They're the ones answering complex questions like, "How can we predict customer sales?"

> ➤ Data Analysts focus on interpreting data and presenting it in a way that stakeholders can understand. They create dashboards, reports, and visualizations.

An easy way to differentiate these roles is to think of a coffee shop analogy:

> ➤ Data engineers set up the coffee machines and ensure they work smoothly.

> ➤ Data scientists create the perfect coffee recipe.

> ➤ Data analysts serve the coffee and explain its flavor profile to the customers.

The Value of Clean, Accessible Data for Decision-Making

Have you ever needed to look for a specific file on your computer and ended up searching through a multitude of folders with confusing names? What if this was on a global level of a company with billions of data sets? Without data engineering, the search and utilization of data would be a disastrous situation.

Data is gold when it is organized and easily obtainable. It enables companies to:

- ➤ Recognise and analyse trends.

- ➤ Adjust their processes in real-time.

- ➤ Create new products and services.

For instance, an omnichannel retailer that is analysing the buying behaviour of customers during the holiday season uses high-quality and integrated data to forecast demand for inventory and enhance the customer experience. A health care system that has patient records as its data requires that the data is correct to facilitate proper diagnosis and treatment.

This is where data engineers come in to contribute in making sure that the data is:

- ➤ Accurate: Free from any form of mistakes or repeated data.

- ➤ Organized: Put in a reasonable and methodical manner.

- ➤ Accessible: Capable of being easily extracted and/or purchased.

When data is organized properly, people will be comfortable using it and this will yield positive results for businesses as well as consumers.

Examples of How Data Engineering Powers Daily Services:

Data engineering is so deeply incorporated in our lives that we often go unnoticed. Here are a few examples of how we rely on it every day:

Logistics and Delivery:

Companies like FedEx and UPS handle millions of packages everyday. Data engineering systems track packages, optimize delivery routes, and identify delays to ensure timely deliveries.

E-Commerce Operations:

Imagine an order placed on Amazon. Behind the scenes, data engineers make sure that inventory is tracked, warehouses are optimized, and delivery times are calculated all in real-time.

Transportation Apps:

Apps like Uber rely on data engineering to match drivers with riders, calculate fares, and optimize routes—all within seconds.

In this chapter, we came to know what data engineering is, how it compares to other data roles, and why it's so critical in the modern world. As we continue through this book, you'll learn how to navigate this exciting field, understand the tools and techniques used by data engineers, and discover how you can become a part of this growing profession.

Key Takeaways:

- ➢ **Laying the groundwork:** Data engineering provides clean, structured, and accessible data, acting as the backbone for modern applications.

- ➢ **Unique responsibilities:** Data engineers focus on building robust pipelines and systems that empower data scientists and analysts to perform their tasks efficiently.

- ➢ **Transformative influence:** Whether it's personalized product suggestions or breakthroughs in healthcare, data engineering is reshaping industries in significant ways.

- ➢ **Teamwork at the core:** By converting raw data into actionable insights, data engineers enable teams to bring innovative ideas to life.

- ➢ **Limitless opportunities:** Learning the fundamentals of data engineering can lead to a career full of exciting challenges and impactful solutions.

Chapter 2

The Data Ecosystem

The data ecosystem is a collaboration of specialized roles mentioned in the previous chapter, each plays an essential part in transforming raw data into actionable insights. Let's explore these roles each in depth to understand how each role contributes to this process.

1. **Data Analyst – The Storyteller:**

   ➤ Data analysts focus on interpreting the data. This helps them in presenting it in a way that stakeholders or the decision-makers can understand. They use various tools like Tableau, Power BI, or Excel to create dashboards and reports that reveal patterns and trends.

   ➤ For example, in a retail company, During the holiday season inventory can be increased based on the recommendation of the analyst who could identify the most popular product categories during a holiday season which makes the owner concentrate on particular product categories and increase the sales.

2. **Data Scientist – The Innovator:**

    ➤ Data scientists push the boundaries of what's possible with data. They use advanced statistical methods, programming, and machine learning to uncover hidden patterns and predict future outcomes.

    ➤ A classic scenario is a ride-sharing app predicting the demand for the ride during peak times. A data scientist analyzes traffic patterns and past ride data to build models that guide drivers to high-demand areas, reducing wait times for customers. Their work connects data and strategy, which enhance the efficiency and user satisfaction.

3. **Data Engineer – The Builder:**

    ➤ Data engineers are the architects of the data world. They design, build, and maintain the systems that store, process, and deliver data. Without them, data analysts and scientists wouldn't have reliable data to work with.

> ➤ For instance, in an e-commerce company, data engineers create pipelines that collect consumer browsing behavior, purchase history, and product inventory data. This data is kept in a clean and structured way where analysts can track trends and sales performance while data scientists use the clean, structured data to develop personalized product recommendations.

Together, these roles form the backbone of the data-driven economy. Their collaboration is what transforms scattered information into the insights that shape industries.

How These Roles Collaborate to Solve Problems:

In every data driven organization an effective collaboration is very difficult between data analysts, scientists, and engineers. Let's look at real-world examples to see how they work together.

1. **Smart City Traffic Management Example:**

   A country like Singapore is a global leader in managing traffic with the use of data using Singapore's Intelligent Transport System (ITS). Let's see how this system is getting efficient because of the effective collaboration of data professionals.

> **Data Engineer:**

Collects real-time large amounts of data from thousands of traffic cameras, road sensors, and GPS-enabled vehicles across the city. This collected data is processed and stored in a centralized system which is clean and prepared for analysis.

> **Data Analyst:**

Analyzes these data to identify congestion hotspots and traffic flow patterns during peak hours. For instance, they might notice that certain expressways experience higher-than-usual traffic before all adjustments. Using dashboards, they provide useful insights to city planners.

> **Data Scientist:**

Predictive models are built by data scientists to forecast congestion based on weather conditions, public holidays, and historical traffic data. These models suggest dynamic toll pricing and optimal signal timings, which the city uses to reroute vehicles and reduce delays.

Through this collaboration, Singapore has been able to manage traffic flow, enhance the efficiency of public transport and improve the experience of the commuters while at the same time reducing the effects which are adverse to the environment.

2. Personalized Streaming Recommendations Example:

An online streaming platform uses data to deliver optimized viewer engagement and personalized recommendations. Here's how it works when these professionals collaborate to deliver personalized recommendations.

➢ **Data Engineer:**

Collects and processes data from millions of users, such as viewing history, watch duration, and ratings. Pipelines are built by Data Engineers to integrate this data from different devices (TVs, phones, tablets) into a centralized storage system for real-time analysis.

➢ **Data Analyst:**

Sees the viewer behavior to identify trends, For Instance, the popularity of specific genres or how contents are being interacted by users during different times of the day. Dash boards are created by them which highlight these insights for content teams, which helps the content team to guide decisions about new series or movie acquisitions.

> **Data Scientist:**

The Data scientist develops recommendation algorithms that identify what users may like, based on the user's viewing history. They also build models that help estimate the interest of viewers for future shows, which helps the company to determine the effectiveness of the marketing strategies and release dates.

This collaboration makes it possible for each user to have an individualized list of content recommendations that are most likely to interest them, leading to higher levels of user satisfaction and retention as well as informing strategic choices made about its content library.

3. **Challenges in Collaborations:**

> **Data Access and Quality:** Analysts and scientists often face obstacles when data pipelines are incomplete or unreliable.

> **Communication Barriers:** The Goals of Engineers, analysts, and scientists must be aligned and to avoid misunderstandings shared terminology must be used.

> **Iterative Workflows: The Changing of needs from** Analysts and scientists may require engineers to continually refine pipelines.

Successful teams create a culture of communication, respect for each role's expertise, and shared problem-solving.

Busting Myths About Overlaps and Distinctions:

There is always a confusion revolving around the roles because of its overlapping nature. There are many misconceptions for these roles. Let's clarify some common misconceptions:

1. **Myth: Data Engineers and Data Scientists are Same.**

   - ➢ **Reality:** Data Engineers focus on building and maintaining the infrastructure that ensures data flows efficiently and is accessible. Data Scientists develop advanced models and algorithms to solve complex problems and make predictions

2. **Myth: Analysts Only Build Dashboards.**

   - ➢ **Reality:** Data Analyst plays an important role in linking data insights to business decisions. They frequently work with Data engineers to define and redefine the data requirements.

3. **Myth: One Role Can Do Everything.**

   - ➢ **Reality:** Generalists are opted in some organizations but specialized roles are more effective for scaling complex data ecosystems.

By understanding these distinctions, businesses can better allocate resources and define responsibilities within their teams.

Key Takeaways:

1. Unique Roles, Common Goals:

> ➤ Data Analysts, Scientists, and Engineers have unique responsibilities but they must collaborate among themselves to succeed.

2. Real-World Applications:

> ➤ Industries are powered by data ecosystems. Industries such as e-commerce, healthcare, and transportation through seamless teamwork.

3. Continuous Evolution:

> ➤ The field is constantly evolving, with new technologies and methodologies enhancing collaboration and efficiency.

4. Beginner-Friendly Opportunities:

> ➤ With dedication and the right skills, anyone can step into one of these roles and contribute to shaping the future of data.

Actionable Advice:

The important step is to Understand the roles within the data ecosystem. To take next step:

- ➤ Take some good time to reflect on which role aligns with your skills and interests—do you enjoy building systems, interpreting data, or creating predictive models?

- ➤ Explore online courses, blogs, or videos about that role to get a sense of its responsibilities and take actionable steps.

Remember, every expert was once a beginner. The key is to start small, stay curious, and keep learning.

Chapter 3

Data Pipelines Simplified

The Lifecycle of Data:

Data can be messy, unstructured and unusable when it is in a raw form and such data is present everywhere. So, exactly what happens in the life cycle of this data? The lifecycle of data within a pipeline transforms it from unstructured data into structured, useful insights. To make it further simple. Let us see the breakdown of this lifecycle.

> ➤ **Raw Data:** To make it a little easier to understand, Imagine data as a water flowing into a reservoir without any filternations. So this water may contain impurities or sediments which make the water not usable. The same way, raw data comes from different sources like IoT sensors, transac-

tional records. At this stage, it's inconsistent and unstructured which requires processing.

> **Processing and Transformation:** This is the next stage in the life cycle where the data cleaning kick starts. Data is filtered, enriched, and Standardized to make sure it meets the quality. Examples such as removal of duplicate entries, missing values filled, and Standardizing the inconsistent formats.

> **Refined Data:** Once the data is processed it is transformed into an actionable product. It's now stored in databases or warehouses, ready for analysis, visualization, or ready for feeding into machine learning models.

Why Scalability and Reliability Matter:

When the data grows in volume and complexity, pipelines must handle increasing demand while maintaining accuracy. Scalability and reliability are the foundation of robust data systems.

1. Scalability – Handling Growth:

An effective pipeline can grow with the business. For example:

> During a Black Friday sale, an e-commerce platform may experience a ten times increase in

traffic. Pipelines must process millions of transactions without delays. Scalable systems ensure that every transaction is processed smoothly, even during peak demand.

2. Reliability – Consistency Is Key:

Let us consider a healthcare system that is based on real time patient monitoring. A single delay in data delivery could lead to life-threatening consequences. Reliable pipelines make sure that:

➢ Data is delivered accurately, without loss or duplication.

➢ One tool I've found invaluable in my experience is Apache Airflow, which provides detailed task monitoring and alerts. For example, when a task in the pipeline fails, Airflow notifies the team immediately, so they can resolve the issue before it impacts the system.

In my journey as a Data Engineer, I've learned that anticipating scalability and reliability needs early on can save countless hours of troubleshooting later. Whether it's building e-commerce pipelines for peak sales or designing healthcare systems with no room for error, these principles have been game-changers

Real-world case studies:

E-Commerce: Handling Orders and Inventory

In e-commerce, data pipelines play a critical role in ensuring smooth operations, especially during high-traffic events like Black Friday. Here's a simplified scenario of how these pipelines work.

> **Ingestion:**
>
> When customers place orders, data flows in from multiple sources, such as the website, payment systems, and warehouse management tools. For example, every order includes information like the product ID, customer details, and payment confirmation, which is collected in real time. The key challenge here is ensuring no data is lost or duplicated during this process.

> **Transformation:**
>
> Once the data is ingested, it often requires cleaning and validation. For instance, duplicate orders may occur if a customer refreshes the page after checkout. Data pipelines check for such issues, removing duplicates and ensuring every order is unique. Additionally, transformations ensure that the payment status is verified, and the inventory count is updated correctly for each item purchased.

> ➢ **Delivery:**

The refined data is then sent to different systems for action. The warehouse team uses this data to fulfill orders, while the customer-facing system updates the order status in real time, letting customers track their shipment. A small error here—such as a delay in updating inventory—could lead to overselling, which pipelines are designed to prevent.

This example highlights how data pipelines work behind the scenes to create a seamless experience for customers and ensure operational efficiency for business

Fashion Industry: Predicting Trends:

Global fashion brands like Zara use data pipelines to identify emerging trends and optimize inventory to stay ahead in the competitive fast-fashion market.

> ➢ **Ingestion:**

Data from in-store sales, customer feedback, and online shopping trends is collected in real-time. For instance, if specific styles are selling out quickly or customers frequently inquire about certain products, this information is captured to help identify what's in demand.

➤ **Transformation:**

The raw data is processed to ensure accuracy and consistency. Duplicate entries, errors, or incomplete records are cleaned. For example, customer preferences, such as trending colors or materials, might be combined with historical sales data to forecast upcoming trends.

➤ **Delivery:**

Processed insights are shared with design and production teams, enabling quick decision-making. These insights help brands like Zara produce and stock trending items within weeks, ensuring they meet customer demands while minimizing overstock.

To read more about Fashion Brand Zara. Scan the QR

> **Key Takeaways:**
>
> 1. **Understanding Pipelines:**
>
>   Data pipelines transform raw data into actionable assets through ingestion, transformation, and delivery.
>
> 2. **Scalability and Reliability Are Non-Negotiable:**
>
>   Pipelines must grow with demand and consistently deliver accurate data.
>
> 3. **Real-World Applications:**
>
>   From healthcare to smart cities, data pipelines drive innovation across industries.

Chapter 4

Tools of the Trade

Foundations Over Trends:

In the beginning of my journey as data engineer I was so excited to jump directly to learn the hottest tools but over these years with my experience i have learnt While tools are essential, but it's very crucial to understand that they evolve and change over time. However, the foundational concepts behind them remain consistent and form the core of data engineering. To make it simple, Tools are like the brushes and paints of the job, but knowing how to create with them is what leads to success

For example, while tools like Apache Spark and Kafka are popular today, they were preceded by others like Hadoop and RabbitMQ. The foundational principles—distributed computing, parallel processing, data ingestion, and transformation—haven't changed. By keeping your focus on these fundamentals, you'll build a skill set that remains unshakeable no matter which tools dominate the market tomorrow.

Key Foundations and Evolving Tools:

Let's deep dive a little more of the foundational concepts of data engineering and how current tools align with them. Remember, the goal isn't just to know the tools but to understand the principles they implement.

1. **Frameworks: Distributed Computing and Parallel Processing**

   ➤ **Foundation:**

   Distributed computing allows huge datasets to be processed more efficiently by breaking down large tasks into smaller ones and running them across multiple machines. It's like baking a hundred cookies using just one oven would take forever, but spreading the batches across multiple ovens speeds up the process significantly. This approach not only saves time but also ensures that if one oven breaks down, the others can keep running.

   Imagine analyzing streaming data from millions of smart devices in real time. Without distributed computing, it would take hours—or even days—to process this data on a single machine.

With distributed systems, tasks are parallelized, ensuring faster results and fault tolerance.

- ➤ **Current Tools:**

  - ○ **Apache Spark:** This framework is widely used for handling big data workloads. I've seen it in action during batch processing jobs where we needed to analyze terabytes of data within tight deadlines. Spark's in-memory computing makes these tasks faster than traditional approaches.

  - ○ **Apache Flink:** Flink is highly useful for real-time applications. One such example is, its use in financial systems to track stock prices or fraud detection systems where decisions must happen in milliseconds.

- ➤ **Why It Matters:**

Distributed computing isn't just a tool—it's a mindset. Whether you're working with Spark, Flink, or a new tool yet to emerge, understanding the "divide and conquer" approach helps you adapt to any framework. The tools may change, but the foundational principles will always stay relevant

2. Orchestration: Coordinating and Automating Workflows

> ➤ **Foundation:**

Orchestration makes sure that the data pipelines run efficiently and smoothly. To give a simple example, Think of it as a conductor leading an orchestra: every piece of equipment must play in harmony to generate beautiful music. Similarly, orchestration tools schedule tasks, manage dependencies, and monitor pipelines for errors. Without orchestration, pipelines would lack coordination, leading to missed deadlines or incomplete datasets.

For example, imagine a pipeline where raw data is ingested, transformed, and then loaded into a reporting system. If one step fails, the entire process is disrupted. Orchestration ensures such failures are caught, and recovery mechanisms are in place.

> ➤ **Current Tools:**

- **Apache Airflow:** Airflow is a widely used orchestration tool known for its flexibility and visual DAGs (Directed Acyclic Graphs), which provide a clear view of workflows. For instance, a data engineer might use Airflow to automate the nightly processing of sales data, ensuring it's ready for analysis by morning.

- **Dagster:** This tool emphasizes modularity and testing, making it ideal for teams that prioritize robust and reusable workflows.

- **Prefect:** Prefect simplifies orchestration with a focus on cloud-native design, making deployment and monitoring easier for modern teams.

➢ **Why It Matters:**

The orchestration tools you use may change, but the principles of scheduling tasks, handling dependencies, and recovering from failures are foundational. Whether you're using Airflow, Prefect, or a future tool, the goal remains the same: ensure that every part of your pipeline works seamlessly together.

3. Data Storage: Efficiently Storing and Retrieving Data

➢ **Foundation:**

Data storage is very important for any data engineering system. The challenge is to store huge amounts of data while ensuring it can be retrieved quickly when needed. Over the time, storage has evolved from on-premises servers to scalable cloud solutions. However, the core principles of efficient storage like scalability, reliability, and accessibility are always the same.

- ➤ **Current Tools:**

  - ○ **Snowflake:** A cloud-based data warehouse that excels in handling structured and semi-structured data with scalability and ease of use.

  - ○ **Google BigQuery:** Google's fully managed data warehouse, known for its speed and integration with other Google Cloud tools.

  - ○ **Amazon S3:** A versatile storage solution from amazon is , S3 which is a commonly used storage for storing logs, media, and backups.

- ➤ **Why It Matters:**

  Knowing how data storage works helps you weigh factors like cost, speed, and scalability. No matter the tool, whether it's Snowflake or something else, the basics of storing, indexing, and retrieving data efficiently remain essential.

4. Data Processing: Transforming Raw Data Into Insights

- ➤ **Foundation:**

  The process of converting raw data into actionable insights is often termed as Data processing. This process involves cleaning, transforming, and enriching data. The final data will be efficiently used for decision-making. The two main approaches of this processing are:

➤ **Batch Processing:**

Processes data in smaller units, making it ideal for tasks that are periodic like generating weekly or monthly reports or analyzing historical trends. Batch jobs are often scheduled at regular intervals, such as nightly or weekly or sometimes daily based on the requirement. This approach works well when real-time updates aren't required, and accuracy is more important than immediate availability of the data.

➤ **Stream Processing:**

Handles data in real time, making it suitable for applications like detecting fraudulent transactions or monitoring live events. This approach processes data as it arrives, enabling immediate insights and actions. For example, stream processing is used in social media platforms to deliver trending topics or in transportation systems to provide live traffic updates.

For instance, think of transforming messy sales data into a structured format that allows analysts to calculate revenue trends or predict future demand. By organizing the raw data into clear and consistent categories, businesses not only understand their past performance but also identify patterns that guide better decision-making.

Current Tools:

> **Apache Kafka:** Kafka excels at managing real-time data streams, making it ideal for applications like monitoring website activity or transaction logs.

> **Apache Beam:** A versatile framework for batch and stream processing, Beam provides flexibility by working across different execution engines.

> **Spark Streaming:** Extends Apache Spark to handle streaming data, enabling real-time insights.

> **Why It Matters:**

Tools like Kafka and Spark Streaming are the current tools in trend may not be in future, but the need to clean, enrich, and transform data will always be crucial. By knowing the foundations of data processing, you'll always be equipped to turn raw data into meaningful insights, regardless of the tools.

Trends Will Change, Foundations Will Stay:

As the landscape of data engineering evolves, so will the tools. Today, Spark and Airflow are industry standards; tomorrow, new tools may come. However, the foundation like distributed computing, orchestration, storage, and processing will be the heart of every data engineering workflow.

In my experience, focusing on the "why" and "how" behind these concepts gives you the flexibility to thrive in a rapidly changing field. Instead of chasing tools, invest in understanding principles like scalability, reliability, and efficiency.

Key Takeaways:

1. **Foundations Over Tools:**

   Tools come and go, but the principles behind distributed computing, orchestration, storage, and processing endure.

2. **Understand the Core Concepts:**

   Distributed workloads, orchestrating pipelines, efficient storage, and real-time processing form the backbone of data engineering.

3. **Stay Flexible:**

   Learn the "why" behind tools like Spark or Airflow so you can adapt to future technologies without losing relevance.

4. **Keep Building:**

   Tools are just enablers; your expertise lies in understanding how to design scalable, reliable, and efficient systems.

Part 2: The Impact of Data Engineering

Chapter 5

How Data Engineering Shapes Industries

The Quiet Force Behind Innovation:

For many industries when we speak about innovation, data engineering is the back bone. So, it is not just a buzzword; Every time an early diagnosis of a patient or a timely arrival of a shipment, or a budgeting app helps someone save money, data engineering is quietly at work. It connects the raw information with actionable insights, driving decisions that shape industries and touch lives.

In this chapter, let us understand how industries such as healthcare, energy and personal finance are being revolutionized by data engineering. Thus, when you are done with reading this chapter, it will be seen that the principles that you discovered during the learning are not only the technical skills – they are the tools which are solving the real-world problems.

1. **Data Engineering in Healthcare: Aggregating Patient Data for Better Outcomes**

Every second vast amounts of data is getting generated in health care like from patient records and diagnostic tests to real-time monitoring devices. The real challenge lies in improving the outcome of the data from these devices by aggregating, processing, and analyzing this data. Data engineering bridges this gap, enabling healthcare providers to make faster and more accurate decisions.

Example: Wearables and Preventive Care

In recent trends health metrics such as heart rate, activity levels, and blood oxygen are collected using Wearable devices like smartwatches and fitness trackers. A notable example is the Apple Watch, which has saved lives by detecting atrial fibrillation (AFib) through its heart monitoring feature. To shed some light by providing details below on how it happens.

How It Works:

➢ **Data Collection:** Sensors in wearable devices collect raw health related data continuously.

> ➤ **Data Processing:** Real-time pipelines clean and analyze the data to identify anomalies like irregular heartbeats.

> ➤ **Data Delivery:** Alerts notify users or healthcare providers when critical thresholds are crossed, enabling timely interventions.

Impact:

Wearables not only provide personal health insights but also integrate with hospital systems to streamline preventive care and reduce emergency visits. For instance, I came across an article in timesofIndia website, the heart rate feature in Apple Watch worn by a policy researcher in Delhi detected her abnormally high heart rate and alerted her. She sought medical attention and escaped a "close call", as per doctors. The 35 year old woman had an Atrial Fibrillation (AFib) -- a rapid and abnormal heart rhythm. She initially ignored these alerts, considering it as a panic attack due to stress. Since the problem persisted she bought an Apple watch to assess her condition. she reported that if the apple watch not alerted her, she would have not gone to hospital in the middle of the night and lost her life. she informed the doctor everything based on the readings from the apple watch. The doctors administered three deliveries of direct current (DC) shocks (50+50+100 joules) to revive her heart's sinus rhythm. This incident clearly prevented her from entering into the Emergency visit and saved her.

Read more at:
By scanning the
above QR.

Example: Hospital Resource Management

In hospitals Resource management is a complex task involving patient inflow, staff scheduling, equipment allocation, and more. These operations are streamlined by providing actionable insights through real-time and historical data analysis using Data engineering which plays a pivotal role in streamlining these operations. Here's a detailed breakdown of how data engineering improves hospital resource management:

How Data Engineering Solves These Challenges:

Specific Applications

1. **Predicting Patient Inflows:**

   ➢ Busy periods such as flu season peaks or emergency spikes after public events can be predicted by Hospitals by analyzing historical data and current trends. **Example Insight:** A hospital might discover that Mondays see a higher-than-average number of admissions, prompting them to schedule additional staff at the start of the week.

2. **Optimizing Staff Schedules:**

   ➤ To recommend staffing adjustments data engineering systems can use past admission patterns and real-time inflow data.

   ➤ **Example Insight:** If data indicates a quiet period between 2 A.M. and 6 A.M., night shifts can be reduced while maintaining essential coverage.

3. **Managing Equipment Utilization:**

   ➤ Critical equipment that have IoT sensors (e.g., ventilators, X-ray machines) provide real-time usage data.

   ➤ **Example Insight:** If a department consistently underutilized an MRI machine, it can be reassigned to another location facing higher demand.

Impact on Hospital Operations

1. **Reduced Patient Wait Times:**

   Predictive insights ensure staff and equipment are ready when needed, reducing bottlenecks in emergency rooms.

2. **Cost Savings:**

Efficient resource allocation prevents overstaffing, saving operational costs.

3. **Improved Patient Outcomes:**

By ensuring timely access to care and resources, hospitals enhance the quality of treatment and overall patient satisfaction.

2. Finance: Personal Finance and Budgeting

Managing personal finances is one of the most common challenges people face, whether it's tracking expenses, saving for the future, or staying within a budget. Data engineering powers the apps and systems that simplify these tasks, turning financial chaos into clear, actionable plans.

Budgeting Apps: Simplifying Money Management

Apps like Mint, YNAB (You Need a Budget), and PocketGuard have revolutionized personal finance by aggregating and analyzing financial data, offering users a clear view of their spending and savings habits.

How It Works:

> **Data Collection:** The app connects securely to users' bank accounts, credit cards, and investment platforms, ingesting transaction data in real-time.

> ➤ **Data Processing:** The Collected data is cleaned and passed to the Machine learning algorithms which categorize expenses (e.g., groceries, dining, or entertainment) and identify spending patterns.

> ➤ **Data Delivery:** Informed Decisions are made by users by the Insights that are delivered via dashboards, alerts, and personalized recommendations.

Example:

A user sets a monthly dining budget of $200. The app tracks their spending and sends an alert when they've reached 80% of the limit, encouraging them to cut back for the rest of the month. This proactive guidance helps users avoid overspending.

Impact of Data Engineering on Personal Finance:

1. **Accessibility:**

   Budgeting and investment apps make financial literacy accessible to everyone, regardless of income level or expertise.

2. **Personalization:**

   With robust data pipelines, these apps deliver highly personalized insights tailored to individual spending habits and financial goals.

3. Empowerment:

Users gain control over their finances through clear, actionable data, helping them make smarter decisions and build financial confidence.

Real-Life Example: PocketGuard

PocketGuard is a financial management app which uses data engineering to help users avoid overspending by providing a "safe-to-spend" number. This figure is calculated by analyzing income, recurring bills, savings goals, and spending patterns, giving users an instant snapshot of their financial health. This app helps users to budget, track bills and subscriptions, and set financial goals.

> ## Key Takeaways:
>
> I have just added only two Industries as an example to show how data engineering creates the impact in those fields but it is not confined only to these industries. Its principles are universal like scalability, reliability, and real-time insights driving innovation across different fields. Whether it's saving lives, optimizing supply chains, or securing financial transactions, data engineering transforms raw information into actionable solutions.
>
> As you continue learning, remember that mastering these foundational skills opens the door to endless possibilities. No matter the industry, your expertise in data engineering will empower you to create systems that solve real-world problems and shape the future.

Chapter 6

Ethical Responsibilities of Data Engineers

The Role of Ethics in Everyday Data Practices:

Data engineers are usually viewed as the architects of data systems, they also serve as guardians of ethical data use. Every time data is collected, processed, and delivered, ethical responsibilities come into play especially when sensitive information like personal health records or financial data is involved. A single oversight can lead to breaches of trust, legal consequences, or harm to individuals.

In this chapter, we'll explore the challenges data engineers face in handling sensitive data, the importance of using the best practices, and the delicate balance between driving innovation and maintaining ethical responsibility. I will showcase some real-life examples and practical tips to show why building data systems ethically isn't just optional, it's essential.

1. The Challenges of Handling Sensitive Data:

During the data handling data engineers often deal with data such as financial transactions to health records treated as sensitive and personal data. Mishandling this kind of data, whether intentional or accidental, can have severe consequences, including privacy breaches, reputational damage, and legal penalties.

Understanding which data is a Sensitive Data:

Sensitive data refers to information that, if exposed, can harm individuals or organizations. Examples include:

- **Personal Identifiable Information (PII):** Names, Social Security numbers, or contact details.

- **Health Data:** Medical histories, diagnoses, or treatment plans.

- **Financial Data:** Credit card numbers, transaction histories, or income details.

- **Behavioral Data:** Web browsing patterns, location histories, or social media activity.

Example: The Consequences of Sensitive Data Exposure

We need to understand what kind of consequences can happen if the sensitive data is not handled Properly.

Scenario:

A large healthcare provider suffers a data breach where hackers gain access to patient records, including names, medical histories, and billing information.

Impact on Individuals:

1. **Identity Theft:**

   ➤ Hackers can use stolen information to open credit accounts, apply for loans, or file fraudulent tax returns in the victim's name.

   ➤ Victims may face financial losses, damaged credit scores, and years of effort to recover their identity.

2. **Emotional Distress:**

   ➤ Knowing that personal medical information is exposed can cause anxiety, embarrassment, or distrust in the healthcare system.

3. Targeted Scams:

> ➢ Scammers can exploit exposed health conditions to target individuals with fraudulent schemes, such as fake treatments or insurance scams.

Real-World Example:

In 2015, a medical data breach at a U.S. health insurance company exposed the personal data of **78.8 million people**, including Social Security numbers and medical histories. The company faced lawsuits, regulatory fines, and loss of trust, with financial repercussions exceeding **$100 million.**

To read the complete details from wikipedia and CNN please scan the below QR's.

	In wikipedia:
	In CNN Article:

2. Best Practices for Ethical Data Use

Sensitive data must be handled responsibly by implementing ethical best practices. Some of the best practises are:

Data Minimization:

- Only collect the data necessary for a specific purpose. For instance, an app collecting location data should avoid accessing unrelated information like contact lists.

Encryption and Secure Storage:

- Whether Sensitive data is being transferred or it is being stored. Make sure to protect it by Encrypting on both sides. It should remain safe from unauthorized access.

Access Control:

- Provide role-based access control to restrict viewing and modification of sensitive data to authorized personnel only.

Regular Audits and Monitoring:

- Periodically audit systems to find any vulnerabilities and look out for any suspicious activities.

Transparency and Consent:

- ➤ Clearly inform users about how their data will be utilized and secure their explicit consent prior to its collection.

3. Balancing Innovation with Responsibility

When creative innovations are being created by data engineers, they must also take care of the ethical dilemmas that are coming when the new technology intersects with privacy and security. To make it simple let us see one scenarios below:

Targeted Advertising Gone Too Far

To deliver hyper-targeted ads an e-commerce platform uses the browsing data of the user. By doing this the ads follow the users across the internet. This makes the user feel that their privacy is being invaded. For instance, let us assume a user browsing a football shoe in the browser to consider for a purchase. While the user uses the social media app he sees the ads about the football. This makes the user feel that he is being watched.

- ➤ **Ethical Dilemma:** How much data collection is too much? At what point does personalization become intrusive?

> **Resolution:** The platform can anonymize user data and provide opt-out options for personalized ads, ensuring a balance between user privacy and business goals.

The Role of Data Engineers

> Data engineers are not only system architects; they are ethical stewards responsible for ensuring that the data systems:

- Respect user privacy.

- Avoid harm or discrimination.

- Balance innovation with accountability.

4. **The Importance of Transparency in Building Trust**

   Transparency is one of the keystones of ethical data engineering. Users are more likely to trust systems that are upfront about how their data is handled. This trust benefits both individuals and organizations.

Key Takeaways:

Ethics as a Core Responsibility:

- ➤ Beyond the technical expertise, a data engineer makes sure that their work upholds privacy, security, and fairness.

Balancing Act:

- ➤ Innovation must be ethical. It's important to be clear and honest and give users control over their data. User must know how their data is being utilised.

Scenarios Teach Real Lessons:

- ➤ Addressing dilemmas in targeted advertising highlights the importance of thoughtful decision-making.

Building Trust:

- ➤ Trust is formed when there is transparency which is benefiting both individuals and organizations in the long term.

We alway used to hear this Dialogue "Great Power comes with great responsibility", Data engineers hold the power to shape how data impacts society. They can guarantee that their work is beneficial to individuals and communities without compromising trust or security by following ethics alongside innovation. This is why you should remember: Ethical engineering is not only good practice, it is the foundation for a data driven future that works for everyone.

Chapter 7

The Future of Data Engineering

What Does the Future Hold for Data Engineering?

In today's digital economy one of the growing fields is data engineering which is becoming one of the most dynamic and essential fields. Ten years ago, data engineering activities were about creating pipelines to move and transform data for reporting purposes on a basic level. Today, it has expanded into a Diverse field that touches real-time analytics, artificial intelligence (AI), machine learning (ML), and even ethical considerations like privacy and security.

Advanced data engineering practices like real-time insights, personalized recommendations, and predictive models are all the Businesses want in recent trends.

The future of data engineering is evolving, so it is not just "building pipelines" any more. For innovations, data engineering is becoming an essential one, which helps organizations make faster and more informed decisions. For instance:

- ➤ Financial institutions are detecting fraud in milliseconds.

- ➤ Healthcare providers are monitoring patient vitals in real time.

- ➤ Retailers are offering instant product recommendations tailored to your preferences.

This evolution means that data engineers are not just problem solvers; they are innovation drivers, shaping the way businesses and industries operate.

Why Should You Care About Emerging Trends?

Data is becoming essential to modern society, influencing all industries from how we shop to how we receive medical care. Companies that use data that are generated by every click, swipe, or transaction, to understand behaviors and improve experiences. Let's see on some daily scenarios:

- ➤ **Shopping Recommendations:** Ever noticed how Amazon suggests products you might like? That's data engineering at work, enabling real-time analysis of your browsing and purchase history to make tailored suggestions.

➢ **Healthcare Monitoring**: Wearable devices like the Apple Watch track heart rates and other health metrics, sending this data to healthcare providers for early detection of issues.

➢ **Smart Cities**: Urban areas are using sensors and real-time data processing to optimize traffic flows, reduce energy usage, and improve public safety.

These examples illustrate how deeply data engineering is already integrated into our lives. When you understand and stay current with the latest trends, then you are not only relevant but also positioned as a key contributor to innovation. Whether you are a beginner in this field or someone looking to advance your skills, knowing where data engineering is heading puts a strategic advantage at your disposal.

This chapter comes alongside three major trends that will define the future: real time data processing, integration of AI, as well as increasing importance of governance and security. These trends will not only define the next generation of data engineering but also unlock new opportunities for those willing to adopt them.

1. ## Real-Time Data Processing

   Real time data processing is not a luxury anymore, it is a necessity. Previous systems were batch data processing systems where data was collected over a period, processed and insights delivered with a lag. This worked for static business models, but in the fast paced digital economy of today, instant insights are needed.

   For instance, when you place an order with a delivery app, the system informs the restaurant, assigns a delivery partner, and tracks your order in real time. This simple process is all made possible by real time data processing.

   ### Why Real-Time Matters

   Real-time data processing allows businesses to act on information as it happens. Whether it's detecting fraudulent transactions in banking, providing personalized recommendations in e-commerce, or ensuring safety in autonomous vehicles, the ability to process and analyze data instantly creates significant competitive advantages.

2. ## Rise of AI and Machine Learning in Data Pipelines

   Data Engineering is being reshaped by AI and machine learning (ML). These make workflows faster, smarter, and more reliable. Manual Efforts by data engineers are required in the traditional tasks like cleaning data or identifying errors. Now, data engineers can focus on higher-value activities where AI can automate these processes.

Use Cases where AI can Help Data Engineers:

➤ **Automating Data Cleaning**: AI tools can detect and fix inconsistencies in data, such as missing values or duplicates. For example, a retail company might have customer names spelled differently across multiple records. AI can unify this data automatically.

➤ **Predictive Insights**: Machine learning models can predict future trends, like a spike in online sales during a holiday season, helping businesses plan ahead.

➤ **Anomaly Detection**: AI can spot unusual patterns in data, such as unexpected spikes in website traffic that could indicate a cyberattack.

Ethical Considerations

While AI makes data engineering powerful, it's essential to use it responsibly. For example:

➤ Avoid biases in ML models that might unfairly favor or disadvantage certain groups.

> Be transparent about how AI-driven decisions are made, especially when they impact people directly, such as loan approvals.

3. Data Governance and Security

With the increasing use of data comes greater responsibility. Data governance and security are key things to ensure that information is managed ethically and securely. To make it simple, data governance is like setting rules for a game, ensuring everyone plays fair, while data security is like protecting the game from being disrupted by outsiders.

Why It's Important

Every time you use an app or make an online purchase, your data is collected. Without proper governance, this data could be misused or exposed to hackers. Regulations and privacy acts were introduced to ensure companies handle personal data responsibly.

Key Aspects of Data Governance

> **Ownership:** Defining who owns the data and who can access it.

> **Quality:** Ensuring the data is accurate and reliable.

Simple Security Practices

> **Encryption:** Think of encryption as locking your data with a secret code, ensuring only authorized people can access it.

> **Access Controls:** Restrict who can view or modify sensitive data.

> **Regular Audits:** Periodically checking systems to ensure data is secure and governance rules are followed.

Real-Life Examples

> **Healthcare:** Hospitals protect patient data with strict governance frameworks, ensuring sensitive information isn't exposed.

> **E-commerce:** Online retailers encrypt payment details to prevent cyberattacks.

Key Takeaways:

1. **Real-Time Data Processing**

   ➢ **Key Insight:** Real-time data processing has become a cornerstone of modern data engineering, enabling businesses to act instantly on live information.

   ➢ **Practical Application:** Industries like finance, e-commerce, and healthcare rely on real-time analytics for fraud detection, personalized recommendations, and patient monitoring.

   ➢ **Getting Started:** Begin by understanding the basics of streaming data and tools like Apache Kafka, which simplify real-time data movement and processing.

2. **Rise of AI and Machine Learning in Data Pipelines**

   ➢ **Key Insight:** AI and ML are transforming data pipelines by automating repetitive tasks, improving efficiency, and enabling predictive insights.

   ➢ **Practical Application:** AI is used for tasks like anomaly detection, data cleaning, and real-time personalization in industries such as retail and entertainment.

> ➤ **Getting Started:** Explore beginner-friendly AI tools and frameworks like Python's scikit-learn or TensorFlow to understand how ML can complement data engineering workflows.

3. Data Governance and Security

> ➤ **Key Insight:** With the growing importance of data privacy and regulatory compliance, data governance and security are non-negotiable for modern data engineering.

> ➤ **Practical Application:** Data governance ensures data is managed responsibly and securely

> ➤ **Getting Started:** Focus on learning the basics of data privacy and governance frameworks, and explore tools.

Part 3: Foundations and Mindsets for Data Engineering

Chapter 8

Building a Data Engineering Mindset

Cultivating the Engineer's Mindset:

Data engineering is actually a mindset. It is a combination of solving problems, curiosity and thinking strategically. It is not just about writing code or using tools. This mindset helps the engineers to develop the scalable systems which solve real-world problem and enable teams to make data-driven decisions

In this chapter we will discuss what it means to have a data engineering mindset. Through practical exercises, real world analogies and actionable insights you will learn how scalability, collaboration and critical thinking form the foundation of successful data engineering. By the end you will see that the skills you build as a data engineer apply far, not just to pipelines, but to how you approach every challenge in your work.

1. Problem-Solving and Critical Thinking: The Core of the Role

Any field whether it's software Engineering or data engineering, tools and technologies will change, but the ability to solve problems and think critically remains an irreplaceable skill. Data engineers will face challenges that are ranging from debugging pipelines to integrating data from various sources. The success lies in how viable you'll be able to break down these issues, analyze their root causes, and develop scalable solutions.

Breaking Down Complex Problems:

Any problem if you see its outer structure it looks unsolvable but if you break them into tiny parts you feel that you could have done this approach in the very beginning stage.

➢ **Example:**

Suppose you're asked to design a pipeline to ingest data from multiple sources and deliver clean, transformed data to a dashboard. Instead of tackling it all at once, break it into phases:

1. Identify the data sources.

2. Choose an ingestion method (e.g., batch or streaming).

3. Define the transformation logic.

4. Design the data delivery mechanism.

This modular approach ensures clarity helps you to complete it without any deviations or troubles.

Developing a Critical Thinking Mindset:

With problem-solving, critical thinking goes hand in hand. It's about analyzing a situation from multiple perspectives, questioning assumptions, and validating conclusions.

i) **Ask the Right Questions:**

A curious, questioning mindset is essential for uncovering the root causes of problems.

> **Key Questions:**

- What's the end goal of this pipeline?

- What potential bottlenecks could arise?

- What happens if the data volume doubles overnight?

ii) Think Systematically:

> ➢ Data engineering involves systems that are inter-connected. Changes in one part of the pipeline can ripple across others. For instance, A change in the schema of a source database could cause errors in downstream processes. We should Anticipate these impacts to ensure system stability.

iii) Iterate and Improve:

> ➢ Whatever may be the Solutions we create, it often needs refinement. Start with a prototype, test it, gather feedback, and improve iteratively.

Real-World Example: Optimizing a Broken Pipeline:

Imagine you're tasked with fixing a pipeline that's running slower than usual. The steps might include:

1. **Identifying the Problem:**

> ➢ Use monitoring tools to locate the bottleneck. Is it in data ingestion, transformation, or delivery?

2. **Diagnosing the Cause:**

> ➢ Investigate whether the issue is due to increased data volume, inefficient code, or resource constraints.

3. Implementing Solutions:

> ➤ Optimize queries, increase processing capacity, or partition data to improve efficiency.

Why Problem-Solving Matters

As a data engineer, your ability to solve problems efficiently affects everything from system performance to business outcomes. By cultivating a problem-solving mindset, you'll not only excel in your role but also become a valuable resource for your team and organization.

2. The Importance of Collaboration in Cross-Functional Teams:

Data engineering is a team effort. Even Though technical skills are essential, what keeps successful data engineers stand apart is their ability to collaborate with cross-functional teams. From data scientists and analysts to product managers and business leaders, a data engineer's work often bridges the gap between raw data and actionable insights. Understanding the perspectives of others and working together toward shared goals is critical for delivering impactful solutions.

In this section, we'll explore the importance of collaboration, the challenges it presents, and practical ways to become an effective team player as a data engineer.

i) **Why Collaboration Matters**

Sitting at the intersection of technical infrastructure and business goals, data engineers must collaborate to ensure the systems they build are not just functional but also impactful.

Aligning with Business Objectives

One thing I've learned in my data engineering journey is that even the most technically flawless pipeline can miss the mark if it doesn't serve the organization's goals. Imagine building a pipeline that processes customer data in record time, but the marketing team still struggles to get the segmentation insights they need. The result? Frustration and wasted effort.

Here's a relatable example: A marketing team might be planning a campaign to target specific customer groups. They need data like purchase history and browsing patterns to make informed decisions. By collaborating with them, a data engineer can understand these requirements upfront and design the pipeline to deliver exactly what's needed, saving everyone time and energy.

Enhancing Data Usability

Collaboration isn't just about meeting immediate needs—it's about making data more accessible and usable for everyone downstream. Data engineers who take the time to engage with data scientists and analysts gain a deeper understanding of how raw data is transformed into actionable insights.

Let me share a real-world scenario. Picture a data scientist building a machine learning model to predict customer churn. They need the data in a specific format—perhaps with certain columns aggregated or filtered. An engineer who works closely with them can preprocess the data in the pipeline, ensuring it's ready to use. This not only saves time but also improves the quality of the final model.

The Benefits of Collaboration:

When data engineers collaborate effectively with cross-functional teams, the benefits ripple through the organization:

➤ Collaborative pipelines deliver data that is more relevant, accurate, and actionable.

➤ Close communication minimizes rework and ensures smoother workflows.

➤ Working with diverse teams broadens your perspective and strengthens your problem-solving skills.

Collaboration is more than just a soft skill—it's a critical competency for data engineers. By aligning with business objectives, and communicating proactively, data engineers can become indispensable team players. Whether you're designing a pipeline, troubleshooting a system, or discussing requirements, remember that the best solutions are built not in isolation but through teamwork.

3. **Scaling Principles: Lessons from Pipelines to Life**

For an effective future whether it's a business or Data engineering according to me, scalability isn't just a nice-to-have—it's a must-have.

Scalability is about preparing your systems for the future, not just solving today's problems. A pipeline that works perfectly for a few thousand records today should also handle more volume a year from now or even more. It's like building a bridge: you don't just build for the traffic it gets now; you think about how much it'll need to handle as the city grows.

The beauty of prioritizing scalability is that it saves you a lot of trouble down the road. Imagine not having to pause your projects to rebuild a pipeline or troubleshoot performance issues because you thought ahead. In my experience, the time and effort you invest in making a system scalable always pays off in the long run.

I'd like to share an experience from my journey. We built a pipeline in Airflow, and at one point, we received a unique requirement: occasionally, a very large file would need to be processed. For these rare instances, the system required additional memory to handle the large file, but upgrading memory permanently wasn't practical. Most of the time, the extra resources would remain unused, leading to unnecessary costs.

To address this, we designed the pipeline to be configurable. When a large file is encountered, the system generates an alert indicating that the file cannot be processed with the current configuration. The support team can then step in and provide upgraded memory parameters to process the file. This was made possible by the parameterized design of the pipeline, which allowed us to dynamically adjust resource allocation only when necessary.

Scaling Systems: Building for the Future

i) **Design for Growth:** A system handling gigabytes of data today should be ready for terabytes tomorrow. This requires foresight and careful design.

> **Example:** A streaming platform might start with 1 million users but must prepare for traffic spikes during a hit show's release. A scalable architecture ensures the system doesn't crash.

ii) **Efficient Resource Management:** Scalability isn't just about capacity—it's about efficiency. Distributed computing frameworks like Apache Spark allow engineers to process large datasets without overloading resources.

Scaling Yourself: Personal and Professional Growth

1. **Lifelong Learning:**

Stay curious and adaptable. Tools and technologies change, but core principles like distributed computing and ETL (Extract, Transform, Load) remain constant.

> **Practical Advice:** Set a goal to learn one new technology or framework every quarter. For example, explore orchestration tools like Airflow or workflow management systems like Prefect.

Key Takeaways: Building a Data Engineering Mindset

1. **Critical Thinking and Problem-Solving:**

   ➢ Break down challenges, ask the right questions, and approach solutions iteratively.

2. **Collaboration is Essential:**

   ➢ Work with cross-functional teams to ensure pipelines meet both technical and business goals.

3. **Think Long-Term with Scalability:**

   ➢ Design systems that grow with future needs and prioritize efficiency.

Becoming a Resilient Data Engineer:

Developing a data engineering mindset means thinking critically, collaborating effectively, and designing for the future. It's not just about solving problems but about anticipating them and creating solutions that last. With the right mindset, you'll not only excel as a data engineer but also contribute meaningfully to the teams and organizations you support.

Chapter 9

Setting the Foundation for Your Journey

Every great journey starts with a strong foundation. For aspiring data engineers, understanding the core principles and appreciating the impact of this role are the first steps toward building a rewarding career. This chapter we are going to focus on simplifying foundational concepts, highlighting how data engineering shapes businesses and society, and inspiring you to stay curious and continuously learn as you embark on this path.

Understanding Foundational Concepts Without Technical Jargon

Designing the system which collects, processes and delivers data efficiently are the core of Data engineering. While the technology may evolve, the underlying principles remain constant.

Core Concepts Simplified:

1. Data Pipelines:

➤ Think of a data pipeline as a factory assembly line. Raw data enters at one end, undergoes transformations (like cleaning and organizing), and emerges at the other end as something usable, much like a finished product.

2. ETL (Extract, Transform, Load):

➤ ETL is the process of taking data from one place (extract), cleaning and formatting it (transform), and delivering it to another location (load).

3. Scalability:

➤ A system's ability to handle growth, whether it's a sudden increase in data volume or new business requirements, is critical to its success.

By breaking these concepts into relatable analogies, you can understand the essence of data engineering without being worried about technical jargon.

2. Exploring the Role's Impact on Business and Society

Data engineering is a behind-the-scenes role, but its influence is everywhere, from personalized recommendations to life-saving medical insights.

Impact on Business:

1. **Efficiency and Decision-Making:**

   ➢ Businesses rely on data to make strategic decisions. Without well-structured pipelines, this data would remain inaccessible, leading to delays and missed opportunities.

2. **Customer Experience:**

   ➢ Data engineers power personalization engines that deliver tailored recommendations in e-commerce, streaming, and travel industries. These systems enhance user satisfaction and drive revenue.

Impact on Society:

1. **Healthcare and Safety:**

   ➢ In healthcare, data pipelines enable real-time monitoring of patient conditions and early diagnosis through wearable devices.

2. **Sustainability and Environment:**

   ➢ Smart cities use data engineering to optimize energy consumption, reduce waste, and manage traffic, contributing to a sustainable future.

Data engineers don't just build systems; they drive innovation and make a real difference

Embracing a Growth Mindset:

Your journey in data engineering will be full of opportunities to learn, grow, and make an impact. Here are some timeless principles to keep in mind:

Timeless Principles of Data Engineering

1. **Focus on Foundations:**

   ➢ Master the principles of data processing, scalability, and pipeline design, as these are the bedrock of the field.

2. **Adapt to Change:**

   ➢ Tools and technologies evolve, but a strong foundation will help you adapt to new paradigms with ease.

3. **Embrace Collaboration:**

   ➢ Data engineering thrives on teamwork. Work closely with analysts, scientists, and business teams to deliver systems that align with organizational goals.

Steps to Stay Curious and Keep Learning

1. **Engage with the Community:**

   ➢ Join forums, attend meetups, and connect with other data professionals to exchange ideas and stay updated.

2. **Build Projects:**

   ➤ Apply what you learn by creating your own pipelines, working on open-source projects, or contributing to community-driven initiatives.

3. **Read and Experiment:**

   ➤ Follow blogs, attend webinars, and experiment with new tools to broaden your skill set continuously.

Conclusion

Embracing the Journey Ahead

As we reach the conclusion of this book, it's important to reflect on the journey we've taken together. From understanding the foundations of data engineering to exploring its practical applications and ethical responsibilities, we've laid the groundwork for your growth in this exciting and ever-evolving field. This book was designed not only to teach you the technical aspects but also to inspire a mindset that drives innovation, collaboration, and lifelong learning.

A Field That Transforms Businesses and Lives:

Data engineering is more than a technical discipline, it's a force that shapes industries and impacts lives. Whether enabling real-time health monitoring, delivering personalized shopping experiences, or powering the next generation of AI-driven technologies, data engineers play a pivotal role in building a data-driven world. The work you do as a data engineer will influence decisions, improve efficiency, and contribute to meaningful change.

Key Lessons to Carry Forward

1. **Foundations First:**

   ➤ The principles you've learned scalability, collaboration, and problem-solving are timeless. They form the bedrock of every successful data engineer's career.

2. **Stay Adaptable:**

   ➤ Tools and trends will come and go, but a strong grasp of the fundamentals will allow you to navigate and thrive in an ever-changing landscape.

3. **Impact Beyond Pipelines:**

   ➤ Your work is not confined to systems and processes; it's about delivering value, solving problems, and enabling others to make informed decisions.

Final Thoughts: Build, Learn, Impact

As you close this book, take a moment to envision your role in the broader data ecosystem. Imagine the systems you'll build, the innovations you'll enable, and the lives you'll impact. Data engineering is more than a career—it's a calling to create, solve, and inspire.

Your journey ahead is filled with opportunities, and you now have the foundation to seize them. So, go forth and build the future. The world runs on data—and you're the engineer who makes it all possible.

The world runs on data, and
Data Engineers hold the keys to its potential.
The journey begins with you.

Thank you

Writing this book has been an incredible journey, and I am deeply grateful to everyone who has been a part of it.

First and foremost, I want to express my heartfelt appreciation to my family. Your unwavering support, patience, and encouragement have been my greatest source of strength throughout this process. Thank you for believing in me and for giving me the time and space to bring this vision to life.

A special thank you to my readers—whether you are new to this subject or an experienced professional, your curiosity and eagerness to learn inspire me. This book is for you, and I hope it adds value to your journey. Your support, feedback, and engagement mean the world to me.

To those who have contributed directly or indirectly— editors, proofreaders, designers, and everyone who played a role in bringing this book to completion—thank you for your dedication and expertise. Your efforts have helped shape this book into something I am truly proud of.

Lastly, I am grateful for the process itself—the lessons learned, the challenges faced, and the growth experienced. Writing this book has been both an enlightening and humbling experience, and I look forward to continuing this journey with all of you.

With deepest gratitude,
Rakesh G

Thank you